# FUN AND GAMES

# Food Shapes

2-D Shapes

John Leach

## Consultants

**Colene Van Brunt**
Math Coach
Hillsborough County Public Schools

**Publishing Credits**

Rachelle Cracchiolo, M.S.Ed., *Publisher*
Conni Medina, M.A.Ed., *Managing Editor*
Dona Herweck Rice, *Series Developer*
Emily R. Smith, M.A.Ed., *Series Developer*
Diana Kenney, M.A.Ed., NBCT, *Content Director*
June Kikuchi, *Content Director*
Susan Daddis, M.A.Ed., *Editor*
Karen Malaska, M.Ed., *Editor*
Kevin Panter, *Senior Graphic Designer*

**Image Credits:** all images from iStock and/or Shutterstock.

Library of Congress Cataloging-in-Publication Data

Names: Leach, John, 1990- author.
Title: Fun and games : food shapes / John Leach.
Other titles: Food shapes
Description: Huntington Beach, CA : Teacher Created Materials, [2018] |
    Audience: K to grade 3. | Includes index. |
Identifiers: LCCN 2017055026 (print) | LCCN 2018000918 (ebook) | ISBN
    9781480759862 (eBook) | ISBN 9781425856922 (pbk.)
Subjects: LCSH: Shapes--Juvenile literature. | Food--Juvenile literature.
Classification: LCC QA445.5 (ebook) | LCC QA445.5 .L4275 2018 (print) | DDC
    516/.15--dc23
LC record available at https://lccn.loc.gov/2017055026

**Teacher Created Materials**
5301 Oceanus Drive
Huntington Beach, CA 92649-1030
www.tcmpub.com

**ISBN 978-1-4258-5692-2**

# Table of Contents

Shapes You Can Eat . . . . . . . . . . . . 4

Start the Day with Shapes . . . . . . . 6

More to Eat . . . . . . . . . . . . . . . . . . 10

World of Shapes . . . . . . . . . . . . . . . 18

Problem Solving . . . . . . . . . . . . . . . 20

Glossary . . . . . . . . . . . . . . . . . . . . 22

Index . . . . . . . . . . . . . . . . . . . . . . . 23

Answer Key . . . . . . . . . . . . . . . . . . 24

# Shapes You Can Eat

You can see many shapes around you.  They are in the classroom and in your home.  They are inside and outside.  They are even in the foods you eat!

# Start the Day with Shapes

You can see shapes at breakfast. What shape do you see?

A **circle** is round and flat. A pancake is shaped like a circle. An orange slice is shaped like a circle, too.

Do you see **rectangles** at breakfast? A rectangle has four **sides** and four equal **angles**.

Look at a pastry. Look at a cracker.

# More to Eat

You might see a **square** in your meal. A square has four equal sides and four equal angles.

A sandwich can be shaped like a square.

Snack foods have shapes, too! Look at these snacks.

**A.**

**C.**

**B.**

**D.**

1. Which snack is an example of a square?

2. Which snack is an example of a rectangle?

3. Draw a closed four-sided shape that is not a rectangle or a square.

A triangle has three sides. The sides form three angles.

A slice of pizza is shaped like a triangle. A slice of melon can be shaped like one, too!

Jen makes this new shape with 4 ham slices.

1. What shape is each ham slice? How do you know?

2. What new shape does Jen make with 4 ham slices? How do you know?

What about dessert?
Look at a pie. A whole
pie is shaped like a
circle. A slice of pie is
shaped like a triangle.

Cookies can be many shapes. Use a cookie cutter on the dough. Make a square. Make a **trapezoid**. Then, decorate them. They all taste great!

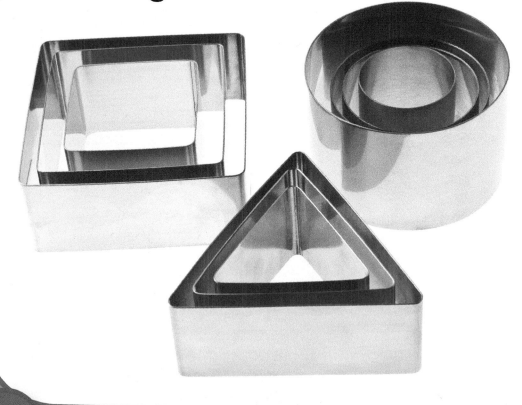

# World of Shapes

Food comes in many shapes. Have a circle for breakfast. Have a square for lunch. Shapes have never been so tasty!

Nina has a piece of flat bread that is shaped like a rectangle. She wants to share it with her friend. She cuts the bread into two smaller shapes.

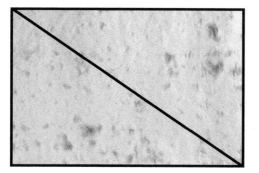

1.  What smaller shapes does Nina make?

2.  Draw a different way Nina can cut the bread into smaller shapes.

# ⚙️ Problem Solving

Cho eats lunch at school. Use her tray of food to solve the problems.

1. What shape is each kind of food?

2. Cho rearranges her sandwich to make a larger triangle. Draw a picture to show how she did this.

3. Draw two different ways Cho can cut her brownie into smaller shapes.

A.

B.

C.

D.

E.

# Glossary

**angles**—corners formed when two lines or sides meet

**circle**—a closed, round shape

**rectangles**—closed four-sided shapes with opposite sides equal

**sides**—parts of lines that form shapes

**square**—a closed shape with four equal sides and four equal angles

**trapezoid**—a closed four-sided shape with one pair of parallel sides

# Index

angles, 9–10, 12

circle, 6, 15, 18

rectangles, 9, 11, 19

side, 9–10, 12

square, 10–11, 16, 18

trapezoid, 16

triangle, 12, 15, 20

# Answer Key

## Let's Do Math!

### page 11:

1. A

2. D

3. Drawings will vary. Example:

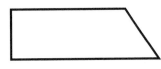

### page 13:

1. triangle; 3 sides and angles

2. square; 4 equal sides and angles

### page 19:

1. triangles

2. Drawings will vary. Example:

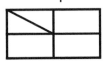

## Problem Solving

1. **A:** circle;
   **B:** square;
   **C:** rectangles;
   **D:** square (2 triangles);
   **E:** triangles

2.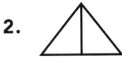

3. Drawings will vary. Example:

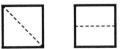